PIMPILICIOUS, OR NOT?
KINGS OF PIMPS
AND KINGS OF POP?

WERE THE TOTALLY UNDISPUTED
KINGS OF POP ALSO KINGS OF PIMPS?

Author: Eric Culpepper

Publisher: In The Wind Productions

Copyrighted Material

ISBN: 978-1-4515227-6-1

ISBN: 1-4515227-6-2

CONTENTS

CONTENTS

CONTENTS

CONTENTS

CONTENTS

CONTENTS

DEDICATION

This analytical work is dedicated to the memory of both Prince and Michael Jackson, artists whom I am completely convinced were 100,000% truer than true plenipotentiary level master pimps who captured our souls, completely warped our entire concept of reality, immortalized themselves in our subconscious minds, transcended all ranks and ultimately achieved deification.

For those of us who were aboard the wondrous ride as Prince' and Michael Jackson's meteoric stars rose and shone so brightly that they lit the entire world, every step of the way we felt as though we were right there with them singing every compelling song, nailing every step of each and every stellar performance, receiving every grand award, selling out every stunning concert and completely shattering every sales and attendance record recorded on the planet. Side by side we truly rocked the world together. Rocking with you was a life altering experience that we shall never forget.

Those who knew of you loved you and perceived of you as immortal in the most inward depths of their subconscious minds and for as long as those of us who were captured by your spell shall live we will miss you dearly. In your absence there will forever be a hole in our lives longing for your mystifying presence. There is not a single one of us who has been left untouched and unenlightened by your work. After a life of dedicated labor to your global community, I hope that in death you can somehow find the rest and happiness that you were rarely afforded in life.

ABOUT THE COVER

From initial image to final thought this work is steeped in the raw and rarely encountered completely unadulterated Truth About Pimpology.

The image on the front cover is my personal plenipotentiary crest, which bears two spirited lions holding up the crown of the master pimp and the shield which bears the light of light and darkness and my initials Piece of Pimp.

FOREWORD

This book has basically been composed to examine the mysterious parallels between the prodigy of Prince and the strategy of Michael Jackson and to determine whether their steady rise to totally unparalleled meteoric superstardom was merely a major mishap or were the musical boy wonders who evolved into the totally undisputed Kings of Pop at their core in fact extremely high ranking lineage master pimps.

This work was initially titled Pimpology Compressor, and it was intended to be a compressed companion book to its far more in-depth parent work "Pimps: The Raw Truth Grand Inquisitor Level Pimpnological Conclusions." However, after the advent of the shocking and untimely deaths of both Prince and Michael Jackson I felt the need to explore what in fact rested at the core of the influential phenomena that those of us who grew up during their electrifying time will surely never again witness in our lives.

This work initially starts with core pandering philosophies and objectives and then proceeds to definitions of characters and concepts that directly parallel cultures of pandering and prostitution the world over and with that basic understanding of the realities and primary objectives of the highest levels of true plenipotentiary level master Pimpology I will use two sets of twenty five totally incontrovertible points to measure both Prince' and Michael Jackson's behavioral and lifestyle patterns against the behavioral patterns and core primary objectives of true master pimps and in conclusion we will yield the profiles of two highly trained and prodigious plenipotentiary level master pimps.

CRACKING THE VAGINA

True Master Pimps have long been known to be both highly intuitive and highly insightful individuals and as a grand inquisitor level Pimpnological decryptologist I can very accurately and precisely tell you that pimp's super-normal insight and intuition stem largely from pimp's relentless obsession with cracking the vagina.

As strange as it may seem to many, it is a totally insurmountable omen of this life that, if one is able to crack the vagina, then one is likewise able to crack the greatest mysteries of this world in the lengthy and rigorous process.

In my more than three decades of relentless research, observation and meditation I have concluded that DNA is ultimately a highly flexible piece of software that in human skeletal form is a remotely controlled mobile antenna. When one observes that the ilium, which are the two largest bones in the pelvic region, are shaped like a satellite dish and that the vagina has a super-normally large influence on both male and female behavior, in that when a woman is at the height of her reproductive capability both she and the males around her dress and behave far more proactively that they do when a woman is the furthest from the reproductive phase of her menstrual cycle, it becomes irrefutably clear that the vagina is in fact a bio-electromagnetic transmission receptacle.

.

ENGAGEMENT AND CONSUMPTION

It is vital to understand that the hard characteristically pursues and engages the soft and is invariably consumed, entrapped and carried away to certain death by it.

The hard intrinsically seeks to slam into the soft and is invariably structurally weakened by the sheer mass of the soft's particles and being hard and resultantly unable to change its form or sustain fractures within its structure, the hard cannot reform and escape the soft and is inevitably completely consumed and devoured by it.

COMMANDERS AND COUNTEROFFENSIVES

For as long as humanity has existed we have engaged in an endless struggle for control of every aspect of our lives including control of opposing genders and foreign cultures and pandering and prostitution, and subsequently religion, which was a later human development, are an age old part of that timeless quest for control of our environment.

Men have long sought out and developed ways and means of luring and entrapping others and one of the most effective tools to do this has always been women; which makes pandering and prostitution some of the oldest counteroffensive tactics known to humanity.

One of the many functional dimensions of a pimp is a man who uses women as weapons of counter-offense and counter-demoralization. And given that women, who are easily convinced that they are being victimized, have never had a problem luring and entrapping men, a true master pimp's work is invariably all too easy.

WAR: FUSION OR CLASH?

Two parties contest a given matter and as the dispute escalates various options are debated until a unanimously agreed upon solution is finally reached, having decided that the only practical form of recourse is battle preparations are made for engagement.

As the given parties find their way to the place of battle and face off against each other they focus all of their energy and attention towards each other as they prepare to make the inevitable exchange of lives. As the inevitable conflict ensues the two sides, racing swiftly toward each other, spirits fully bared, engage each other in battle they become physically, mentally and spiritually intertwined, at which point it becomes impossible to distinguish the difference between the two.

Observing, one cannot tell the commander from the corporal from the captain. Nor can one distinguish the friend from the foe from the friction and neither will anyone ever be able to again for they have fused and through a combination of observation, assault, rape, reparation and eventual reconciliation those whom were once two halves have been forged into an inseparable whole.

It is a fact, not only of physics but of spirit and conscious as well, that all that is combined is destined to mesh, this is why we have a global economy today because through our massive battles we became spiritually, physically, socially and economically intertwined, and we meshed.

WAR: FUSION OR CLASH?

War is merely a crude syringe that employs shock to deliver various ideologies to and thereby ultimately sedate and restrain a given candidate. However, the danger of warfare is that aggressors are easily led and entrapped, therefore one must be careful not to set oneself up to be countered, stunned, consumed and become an unwitting victim of his own vile addictions.

The true warrior is a winner of souls who seeks not to take lives but to gain spirits and one has not truly gained victory until one has gained the soul of his former enemy.

Victory and defeat in war are not determined by any of a given campaigns battles but by one's final resting position in the aftermath of conflict, therefore it has long been said by masters of warfare that it is possible to win the war and lose the peace; in which case the massive destruction and loss of life have all been for naught.

It is said that one should keep his friends close and his enemies closer.

As mortally destructive as it invariably is, throughout history, war has proven to be one of humanities most galvanizing forces.

VALUE

Crime ultimately doesn't pay in the long term because crime is often carried out by those who have no values and those who value nothing cannot possess anything of value, for they cannot see the value in anything.

FAILURE AND FOCUS

In life, reality is invariably determined by focus, and the total focus of panderers and prostitutes is breaking people and they invariably wind up broke themselves as a direct result.

One is either building or breaking, one cannot do both, for it has long been recorded that one cannot serve two masters.

I feel that it is extremely important, especially for young people, to understand that pandering and prostitution are ultimately a binge, not a glamorous business venture. Pimps and human traffickers are not merely salesmen who deal in flesh, they are extremely unhealthy and irrational individuals who have been victimized their entire lives and are engaged in some degree of self-destructive counter-reactionary binge.

RELIGION

It is absolutely no coincidence that all refined cultures have developed religion and it is equally no coincidence that those varied religions are in many aspects dramatically different from each other exactly as weapons that are ultimately designed to accomplish the same morbid task often differ from each other dramatically.

One cannot have civilization without order, and one of the primary methods that has been devised over the millennia to maintain order within society is the occasional use of restraint and thus is one of the core reasons for the development of religion, out of the need to restrain masses of people without the danger of a totally destructive counteroffensive that could completely collapse a society.

Religion as one of the greatest means of diversion and restraint ever devised by man, I also defined religion as the single most destructive weapon ever devised by man. Religion is the forerunner of many weapons that have been devised after the advent of religion and many of those weapons are in fact by-products of religion and if the average practitioner of any religion knew who was leading them to heaven they'd be scared to go. And Panderers and Prostitutes are an excellent example of this, throughout history true master panderers have invariably emerged from religious centers and religion is the underpinning that gives true master Pimpology and many other aggressive activities their true strength.

THE BIBLE

The Bible, which is in fact the best-selling compilation of books ever composed and one of the most vital literary works ever devised, is ultimately a blue print for global conquest that conveys directions for the construction of a Kingdom that is to break in pieces and consume all of the nations of the world.

The Bible is of importance to pimps at the master level and beyond because it gives many vital clues to human nature and the nature of women, including women who live as whores. The Bible records that a whore's foot is set upon hell. This insight is a core and extremely vital part of what drives whores to act as they do and it is likewise a warning to those who engage whores that if ignored can lead one to misery, hell and certain death at the hand of whores and their likewise hell addicted operatives.

GOOD

As much as people like to look at good, or anything in life, as something that is one dimensional, clear, and firmly fixated, good is in reality largely a matter of perspective.

EVIL

As an individual who has spent a lifetime exposed to that which many would consider to be evil, and as a lineage disciple of masters of a discipline (pimping) that many consider to be evil, I can get into real specifics about what is in fact functioning evil versus that which is in fact mythology.

Evil is ultimately and in core essence merely a gross lack of consideration that inevitably yields disaster and many people who do things that are considered to be evil are often stopped by those who are considered to be good because individuals whom are labeled evil are invariably awesomely inconsiderate and dysfunctional individuals who cannot create even a remote form of balance and since they cannot create extremely vital balance their actions invariably ultimately yield collapse.

CONQUISTADORS

We all know that the Conquistadors were conquerors who savagely massacred millions in their push to found the so-called new world. However, this same conquering spirit has existed as long as there has been life on this planet. The guardians of this world are monsters and in fact people can be broken down into two basic groups: The Aggressive and The passive.

Aggressors, as they apply to what is to follow in this compressed book, will be defined as those who govern and assist in the governing of society in general. The Passive, will be defined as those whom are subject to the governance of the aggressive.

ENFORCERS

Enforcers are individuals who force the laws and determinations of those who govern society upon a society's people, and in functioning reality many of those who fill the ranks of enforcement agencies are merely thugs with government resources, and while some consider this to be a tragedy it is in fact an age old necessary evil.

Who else but thugs are going to catch and stop thugs who are in general the only people who break the law?

CRIME

Crime is merely a form of rebellion or a counteroffensive of sorts in which one group of aggressors is pitted against the empowered group of aggressors and the level of crime within a given society is invariably determined by the level of exclusion, dysfunction and corruption that is forced upon common people by those who govern society.

Epidemics of criminal activity are in core essence cultural problems that generally occur when government is either awesomely corrupt or dysfunctional which invariably causes ordinary people to turn to crime organizations for security which yields a situation in which crime lords are allowed to function in the stead of government officials and lead counteroffensive campaigns to in effect beat the system back. This is a situation that should be avoided at all costs, because regaining control of a given situation from crime lords that have gained control of military and law enforcement invariably ends in a bloody disaster. Having career politicians in control of society is bad enough.

Epidemics of criminal activity invariably require cultural reform to solve them. As a graduate of hell I can tell you that hell can in fact be graduated, this is why we have priests, law enforcement and grand inquisitor pimps.

CAREER CRIMINALS

Career Criminals are merely individuals who have dedicated their lives to beating an invariably corrupt system back. The interaction between thugs and law enforcement agents is in reality a series of actions and counter-reactions between thugs and thugs with government resources, a series of counter-reactions in which it can sometimes become extremely difficult to tell which group is which and who is in fact on which side.

Any truly good law enforcement agent is merely a thug with a conscious and being that enforcers are former non-government thugs themselves criminal activity presents enforcers with what sometimes proves to be over-whelming temptation to fall back into their former way of life.

PREISTS

A Priest (or Priestess) is the furthest evolution of an aggressor, he is an individual whom has transcended general criminal activity to the point that he is beyond the average person's view and consequently above and beyond their realm of suspicion.

I always told my children that a priest is merely a thug who has been refined by religion, which is one of humanities greatest managerial achievements.

Religion is something that I often liken to medicine, which is lifesaving in measured doses, however, in overdose it is pure poison and the same is equally true of religion, which can be exceedingly destructive in the hands of inconsiderate people. This is one of the primary reasons that when religious figures are situated in total control of all areas of government it invariably yields disaster. Religion itself is already an extreme form of restraint, couple that extremity with the extremism of the military and law enforcement and you have an extremely volatile recipe for catastrophic disaster and we have thousands of years of history to show us this. History has shown us time and time again that complete power corrupts completely.

As for how all of this applies to The Truth About Pimpology, many true master pimps emerge from deeply religious families who have direct lineages of evangelism and priesthood and pimps often ascend back into the priesthood themselves after they have graduated attempting to function as pimps.

PREISTS

In the ideological rhetoric of extremely high ranking master pimps it is said that the church emerged from the pimp and the pimp merely entered his grandest creation. True master pimps in fact consider priests to be the furthest evolution of pimps, they consider priests to be anxiety managers and fear salesmen just like themselves. Pimps view priests as the same cats in red and black maintaining a constant state of fear by indirectly threatening people's afterlives for money and the history of the priesthood doesn't do much to refute this seemingly ridiculous claim as priests have been involved with direct parallels of pandering and prostitution throughout their history.

Contrary to popular belief and urban mythology, a pimp absolutely is not in any way, shape, form or fashion a lady's man. In reality, a pimp is merely a counter-reactionary extremist who is the King of a minuscule Kingdom that is built on the mess that other people have created. And as such, panderers are in functional essence commanders of minuscule armies of lovers, they are individuals who drive sexual counteroffensives in which they use misery addict women as lures and sex as a weapon to entrap, counter-demoralize and break people (especially men) in every way imaginable.

Many individuals, especially young men, who claim to want to be pimps are in fact attracted to women and have absolutely no idea of the realities of pandering and prostitution; especially not the fact that whores are not ordinary women but women who are completely obsessed with demoralizing and destroying men.

Contrary to popular belief pimping is not an offensive act as many people who really don't understand exactly what pimping is and what a real pimp in fact does. Pimping is in fact a counteroffensive act, and this fact is a vital part of the reason that pimping is able to draw whores to it. And having absolutely no awareness of pimping's true morbid realities young men who claim to want to be pimps can very easily land themselves in a world of trouble before they are able to see what The Bible records as "The light of darkness."

DEITY LEVEL PIMPS

A deity level pimp is a pimp who has an omni-dimensional level of both capability and comprehension, he is an individual who understands the pimping on such an extremely high level that he is capable of pimping on absolutely anyone or anything at any time without anyone's knowledge; in essence, his pimping is completely undetectable.

Where a base level master pimp works to create a somewhat steady base of often immoral support that allows him to live an often feigned life of leisure, a proper deity level pimp is capable of creating a multi-generational base of support which generally doesn't include women who work as prostitutes and may be accomplished by any one or numerous means of gaining support from generating a consumer base for his products to covertly owning the tax base of a nation or an entire global civilization.

GRAND INQUISITOR LEVEL PIMPS

Grand Inquisitors are invariably lineage theologians who are extremely important individuals whose lives are dedicated to the ceaseless consideration of the laws generally recorded in religious works of all kinds which are basically records of human actions and counter-reactions and through this ceaseless meditation in the law grand inquisitors are able to develop tremendous insight, foresight and effective solutions and are causatively able to develop a highly refined omni-dimensional level of pimping that likewise rarely employs women and is completely undetectable.

PLENIPOTENTIARY LEVEL PIMPS

Plenipotentiary Pimps are master prey, master profilers, master victims, masters of clearly identifying and drawing others into entrapment as opposed to being entrapped themselves. All that any pimp ultimately needs a prostitute for is reach, to have the courage to ask for that which a pimp himself would be denied had he made the request. However, at the plenipotentiary level a master pimp has reached a level of comprehension and capability that he doesn't need to employ women to reach or accomplish his objectives for him, he can either work with or, most effectively, without women.

GRANDMASTER PIMPS

Grandmaster Pimps are able to function as predator predators, they are masters of recognizing, pursuing and preying upon predators. Grandmaster Pimps are also pimps that have transcended the need to employ women to accomplish their objectives for them.

MASTER PIMPS

Masters Pimps are master predators who are masters of profiting from women's lack of control of their anxieties, they are masters of converting individuals who have been victimized their entire lives into highly motivated counter-aggressors. People are not as rational as they are counter-reactionary in nature and understanding this insurmountable fact of life a master pimp is not in search of a piece of the action, but a piece of the counter-reaction.

A true master pimp has a complete understanding of the fact that men are explosive in nature whereas women are implosive in nature, he realizes that men lash out at other people and blame other people for their problems whereas women turn on themselves and blame themselves for their problems, he realizes that men hurt other people to hurt other people whereas women hurt themselves to hurt other people and having a total realization of these morbid facts of life a pimp doesn't pimp on a woman as much as he pimps on her dire needs and uncontrollable anxieties.

Many masters at the street level are adverse psychologists, or what I refer to as hell salesmen. These are individuals who sell an extremely powerful and effective ideology (which is also used very effectively by gangsters) that says that life is a never ending struggle in which one must victimize or be victimized, have or be had, take or be taken, stand up or be stood over, roll or be rolled over and overrun by other people for the rest of their life.

MASTER PIMPS

There is a lot of (especially corporate) victimization out there and what these pimps sell women is merely an augmentation of the cold realities that many people face in their attempt to survive the daily rat race of modern life. And in a highly competitive money driven culture in which strife has absolutely no loyalties and everyone from pimps to policemen to politicians to the presidents of global corporations is trying to claw their way to the top of this massive heap called accomplishment the words of a true master pimp all too often ring all too true. A master pimp has a morbid realization of the fact that modern civilization has basically evolved into a colossal contest in which everyone is trying to gain everything in exchange for absolutely nothing.

A pimp is not a gentleman of leisure as much as he is a master of anger management and pimps ultimately don't function as carefree leisurologists who live lifestyles of lavish luxury, in reality, pimps are far closer to being the Kings of minuscule, dysfunctional and highly unstable Kingdoms that are built on the mess that other people have created; mess that invariably yields a pimp's total collapse.

PROFESSIONAL PIMPS

Professional Pimps are tunnel visionary at absolute best, they are individuals who are professionals of manipulating women into engaging in prostitution. A good professional pimp is highly skilled at isolating individuals from completely unforgiving cultures and driving them to do the totally unforgivable. However, they often lack a complete understanding of the true nature and dynamics of what they are engaged in and they often find themselves entrapped and occasionally even murdered by their women because they don't understand what a whore is and subsequently what her true motivations and ultimate objectives are.

A proper pimp is invariably a lineage theologian and if he is not he is a dead man walking as he is functioning without a real understanding of what he is dealing with or an ability to foresee or devise solutions to anything.

Professional Pimps are players who often play themselves to death. Professional Pimps are quite fond of referring to themselves as cash money hustlers and they are very good at luring women with cash and flashy cars and manipulating women with promises of a glamorous lifestyle financed by whoredom which is sold to women as a source of income that absolutely cannot be depleted. However, the grave danger that professional pimps unwittingly face is that they are mistakenly convinced that all women are weak and can be made whores, they also often believe that whores are women who are sexually attracted to money and by the time that they figure out that these conclusions are in fact grossly incorrect they have all too often fallen mortal victim to the morbid addictions of hell's maidens whose feet are in fact set upon hell exactly as is recorded in The Bible.

100% HUSTLERS

100% Hustlers are in fact not really pimps, as they will hustle on anything that they can get their hands on. And hustlers generally don't understand the true dynamics of being a pimp, but they are so good at conning and manipulating women into doing things, very much including giving hustlers their money and having sex with hustlers and various other people, that they appear to be pimps to those who don't know any better when in fact what people are observing is merely an illusion of pimping.

GUERILLAS

Though in blaxploitation cinema and urban mythology alike individuals who attempt to beat the stuffings out of women are labeled pimps, which is in fact taken as an insult by individuals who in fact are pimps, the reality is that individuals who exhaust and sweat themselves half to death beating women senseless are merely frustrated idiots and as much as people justifiably like to demonize them by calling them pimps in reality they are not pimps. These are individuals who are in reality apparitions of the hideous women who have scarred and victimized them and have invariably been the sole influence in their lives.

I was once in a conversation with some brothers about the true definition of a Mack and a White guy that was present cut in and informed us that we were all wrong... as White guys often do.

"Guys...A Mack is a truck!", the White guy quite whitely informed us... to which I replied... "A Mack will run your a** over like a truck if you let him!"... And he appeared baffled, as though he had happened upon something to contemplate for the rest of his life.

Contrary to popular belief, a Mack is not a pimp or a player...or a truck, for those of you who are White! A pimp is ultimately a master victim who is causatively a master of victimization, and he is in core essence merely a trick who wants a refund. A player is merely a man in derision. However, a true Mack is in fact as close to a lady's man as what are perceived as players come.

A Mack is an individual who is irresistible to women, especially to women who are broken. Given ear, a good Mack can talk a woman into doing absolutely anything.

The Mack likes to believe that he is a lady's man but he is in fact a predator, though he cannot look into the mirror and face this fact.

A Mack is ultimately a man who is hurting deep inside and causatively externally makes near blood sport of hurting and breaking women until he is fortunate enough to find a wonderful woman to save him from himself and his morbid addictions.

That's so beautiful... My God, my eyes are tearing...I better stop before I... before I have to go outside in the rain.

PLAYERS

I hate to sound arrogant, but player is the most misunderstood word in a moron's vocabulary, it ranks right up there with pimp, b**** and whore in the realm of the age old grossly misunderstood. We've all heard people refer to themselves as players and we've all thought of them as morons. And you know what?... Sometimes everyone is absolutely right!

In reality, a player is merely a con artist, an individual who is trying to con his way through life. There is no more to a player than that. A player doesn't have the discipline, guidance or anxiety to be a pimp, he doesn't have the finesse to be a Mack, in fact he doesn't have much of anything at all ...just a not very good line of bullsh**.

WHOREDOM

Whoredom, which is often referred to as the world's oldest profession, is in fact merely a form of counter-reactionary extremism, a form of rebellion that is generally (however, not exclusively) engaged in by women.

We have all heard stunningly ignorant and ridiculous people try to say that all women are whores. However, the reality is that in crude calculation I figure that approximately one woman in fifteen thousand worldwide is a whore if that many and in terms of anxiety, the average lady is no more a whore than the average bottle rocket is the space shuttle, just as it takes an inconceivably tremendous amount of thrust to propel something out of the stratosphere into space it likewise takes an inconceivably tremendous amount of anxiety to propel a woman to true whoredom, to make her truly turn her back on everything that she has ever known in life to pursue her anxieties. Anxiety rules and completely determines every conceivable aspect of a whore's life and she is resultantly driven by anxiety to do what is considered by the average woman to be the unthinkable and whore's inability to gain control of their anxieties all too often costs them their lives.

ROTTEN WHORES

A rotten whore is the most hideous form of woman in existence, often mistaken for a prostitute she in fact is not a prostitute and rarely engages in prostitution. However, she has dedicated her life to the demoralization of other people, invariably even her own parents and children. Unlike a mere whore who is merely out to degrade and break men, a rotten whore is obsessed with breaking everyone. A rotten whore is an exceedingly dangerous and contemptuous individual who is a serial predator who feeds on the pain of loneliness and generally functions solely by herself, as she refuses to allow herself to be buried alive in charges and debt as is required by a pimp.

A rotten whore is an individual who is ultra-dysfunctional and is resultantly so completely isolated that she has no friends or family other than her children whom she incessantly keeps on punishment and tirelessly abuses and employs as weapons. A rotten whore is unable to maintain employment, she has no creditors, she has no stable source of housing or transportation because she has completely destroyed her relationship with her parents by both physically and verbally assaulting them and she is so staunchly opposed to the idea of owing anyone anything that she would rather use public transportation than owe anyone a car note.

A guaranteed tell-tale mark of a rotten whore is that a truly rotten whore is completely obsessed with the idea that everyone is trying to steal from her, she has even often devised alternative methods of calculation because she is completely obsessed with the idea that everyone is out to cheat her and she is very often a veteran employee at bars, night restaurants, rehab programs or anywhere that she can immerse herself in abuse and fulfill her insatiable need for negative energy.

The difference between a standard whore and a rotten whore is that while a standard prostitute sells her body, or since ancient times her head in the form of oral sex to avoid whore's age old paranoid obsession with the idea of being judged by people, a rotten whore, who absolutely can't stand to be touched by anyone, not even her own children, only sells her body as an absolute last resort means of preserving her life.

Whoring is an extremely unnatural act, women are not whores by nature and I estimate that one woman in fifteen thousand world-wide is a whore if that many. However, a truly rotten whore, who is an even more extremely rare one in fifty thousand individuals occurrence, is only concerned with completely destroying people in every way possible and naturally some rotten whores evolve even further into serial killers and though difficult to distinguish from a proper lady because she has the silhouette of a priestess she is easily recognized by a true master, and I have busted many from Toronto to Tennessee.

To the inexperienced eye a rotten whore initially appears to be an ordinary lady who has merely had a few bad experiences in life and is causatively extremely cautious to the point of celibacy. However, the difference between an unfortunate lady and a rotten whore is that while a lady, who often refers to herself as a bum magnet, has a need for men to be monsters, as do many women who are involved in serial exploitive and abusive binge relationships, a rotten whore is different in that absolutely none of the pitch black tales of her life add up.

Unlike an ordinary lady or even a standard whore, a rotten whore generally comes from a stable, supportive and by any measure excellent family environment. However, being a mentally unstable counter-over-reactionary extremist she invariably claims that everyone that she has ever encountered in life has been an exploiter.

A rotten whore is recognizable by the fact that she is a shadow of death in that everything in her circumference is either dead or dying. She can't seem to remember ever having been involved in even a single functional relationship in her entire life, not even with her parents or childhood friends. She is generally by some means visually stunning and is surrounded by exceedingly decent suitors but constantly refuses to have any one of them and chooses instead to pursue a life of ceaseless difficulty and willfully chooses to be celibate to the point of inhumanity.

A rotten whore is an individual whose soul has been gutted by hatred, she is an extremely rare form of introvert. If a woman is inexplicably dysfunctional to the point of total irrationality and won't reach out to anyone for help she has likely evolved into a rotten whore. A whore is not a woman who has a big appetite for sex, but an insatiable appetite for destruction.

A true whore is merely an ordinary woman who is a counter-reactionary extremist, she is a woman who over-reacts to everything, she is not a slut, nymphomaniac, moron or punk as is propagated by commonly accepted guess work and ghetto mythology.

Whores are women who have extremely warped concepts of strength and masculinity and they resultantly take tremendous pride in not giving a d*** about anything in life and they often have a need for men to be monsters. This is in fact one of the core reasons that whores spend years involved in serial abusive and exploitive relationships and it's ultimately why they pay pimps. Whores are in fact willing to pay their lives to have men affirm their extremely warped concepts of masculine reality for them.

In functional essence, the act of whoring goes to the fact that everyone has needs…and this is equally true of women, some women have a need for love and companionship, some women need inspiration and assistance and some women have a need to be thrown off of Sears Tower. Women ultimately act like they're treated and it is in women's nature to relentlessly pursue individuals to help them gain that which they have been made to feel that they deserve.

Many women who function as whores have been torn down and emotionally demolished all of their lives and they resultantly see men as monsters and view life as a cruel contest in which he whom is most heartless is the victor. This is why it is possible for a true master pimp to convince a whore that she is surrounded by predators and life is in reality all about victimization and through well calculated positioning he is able to convince a whore that the world is flat and if she gets too far away from the pimping she will walk right off of the edge of the world. Many people carry this mindset without realizing it.

ARTIFICIAL WHORES

Artificial Whores are in fact women who are made to function as whores but are in general ordinary women who have been entrapped in sexual enslavement or drug addiction. Victims of human trafficking are an excellent example of Artificial Whores, they are ordinary women who have been lured, rounded up or by other means made unwilling victims of sexual enslavement.

NEGLECTED CHILDREN

Neglected Children are children who have generally been abandoned, neglected or directly sold into prostitution by their family and they are generally products of inconceivable levels of family dysfunction. Prostitution rings easily recruit neglected children who are more than willing to engage in survival sex to sustain their lives.

NYMPHOMANIACS

As much as men (very much including myself) hate to admit it, unless an individual is sick themselves anyone who has spent any amount of time with a nymphomaniac can figure out pretty quickly that something is wrong with these individuals. I have experienced relationships with nymphomaniacs myself and I can tell you from firsthand experience that their ability to rationalize is completely non-existent; much like women who are in severe depression.

There was one nymphomaniac that I knew who kept getting involved in extremely unhealthy relationships with individuals who were threatening to kill her if she gave them a sexually transmitted disease. She said that one individual even often joked with her about becoming his whore and she'd wondered if he was really kidding with her or not. As a master pimp, without hearing any more of her story I was able to tell her with total confidence that he in fact was not kidding with her.

"Since you're a nymphomaniac he thought that you were a whore", I told her.

She was an extremely nice lady who absolutely was not a whore, I have been around whores all of my life and she had none of a whores negative energy or morbid obsession with trying to demoralize and break people. After taking a few rides I tried to get her to get some help for herself and a truck load of prophylactics.

NYMPHOMANIACS

The point of this little story is that because nymphomaniacs have insatiable appetites for sex and appear to act like whores to people who don't know any better some people naturally mistakenly think that they are whores when in-fact a nymphomaniac is not a whore, she is a sufferer of depression and severe emotional distress which is being vented through sex addiction.

Just as some unhealthy people eat foods that are filled with ultimately dangerous hormones, steroids and emulsifiers that are already ultra-fattening to make themselves feel better, these unhealthy individuals use sex as a means of self-pacification; and the young lady in question was also quite obese, in the end she proved to be too much of a good thing.

PRESTO-CHANGE-WHORE:
THE RECIPE OF A WHORE

Take a few good doses of irresponsibility, impatience, irrationality, infidelity, child neglect, physical abuse, relentless criticism, family dysfunction, spite, corruption, police brutality, demoralization, depression, ultra-low cost housing, industrial pollution, poisoned vital resources, sodomy, pornography and a sprig of trauma...mix well.

Strain mixture through extreme poverty, ignorance, racism, isolationism, militancy and/or religious extremism.

Add a few teen pregnancies, a couple of failed rehab attempts, a few accusations of two dollar whoredom, a few c-sections with a dull axe, a few nowhere in life at twice the speed of light waitress jobs where you're being subjected to emotional distress and accused of theft by a rundown, rotten, ex-whore of a restaurant manager who is in fact the real thief, a few overdue bills, a few family altercations and a few dreams of escape...allow to simmer.

Add a few bags of weed, a few ocean front property in Arizona-esque awe-inspiringly incredible pipe dreams of starting your own clothing line and traveling the world and meeting the stars as a high paid stellar hoe, a few stories about how you fell and the angry looking black guy who is obviously your pimp is just your ride, a pair of superglued stilettos, a nice gray rat fur coat that has a couple of holes in it, adopt some freaky whore name like midnight angel, private dancer, money box or precious and presto-change-whore, you have the vague beginnings of one condom packin', fast trackin', flat backin', cheese stackin' whore.

PRESTO-CHANGE-WHORE:
THE RECIPE OF A WHORE

Whores are invariably products of cultures in which people take tremendous pride in giving a d*** about absolutely nothing and view and have completely accepted life as a relentless struggle that is all about counter-demoralization and victimization and whores resultantly habitually surrender themselves to and completely entrap themselves within the grasp of predators and panderers.

We cannot hope to effectively manage and diffuse the scourges of pandering and prostitution and human and organ trafficking if we are not at least vaguely aware of some of their core compositional and motivational elements.

PIMPOLOGY, TRICKNOLOGY
AND ADVERSE PSYCHOLOGY

So many people look at pimping from the outside and wonder what a man could say or do to a woman to move her to willingly sell her body for him at the risk of her freedom, her soul, her life, and being an individual who has spent the better part of my life exposed to the game as a ten toes stomp down disciple of its masters I might be able to offer a bit of insight into the intricacies of the game and how it works.

So many people think that pimping is just about rapping and blazing sacks, but here are a few of the facts.

At its core pimping is about drax and sacks and fuzzy facts. Macks and pacts and stunning lacks. Hounds and bounds and copping crowns. Pros and prose and gangster flows. Bro's and snows and cameos. Teens and schemes and silent screams. Fiends and liens and shattered dreams. Screws and shrews and roach's eye views. Blues and lieu's and wrecking crews.

The game entails wile and guile and fast track style. Smiles and files and juveniles. Lures and tours and faux grandeur. Floss and gloss and sequential loss. Jaws and draws and wife-in-laws. Canes and feigns and short-lived gains. Janes and stains and punctured veins. Bones and jones and precious stones. Lies and thighs and bloodshot eyes. Rides and hides and suicides. Rings and stings and licentious things. Fees and B's and stackin' cheese.

PIMPOLOGY, TRICKNOLOGY
AND ADVERSE PSYCHOLOGY

The game is about slaves and braves and finger waves. Fables and stables and cutting tables. Feds and threads and thoroughbreds. Dice and feist and pubic lice. Hate and bait and dropping weight.

Scolds and folds and captured souls. Bars and scars and fading stars. Balls and falls and camisoles. Binge and bash and foil wrapped stash. Bricks and cliques and heinous hicks. Shining, reclining and masterful timing. Sluts and guns and untaxed funds. Bumpin' and rollin' and b****es strollin'. Squirrels and pearls and nether worlds. Brutes and toots and silent flutes. Dumps and bumps and aching pumps. Lines and binds and one track minds. The game offers vice and spice and ice and anything that you like…for a price.

That, boys and girls, is a brief synopsis of what true game is made of. I just haven't figured out why it's called a game yet, cause ain't nobody out there playing.

For those inclined to pop that wine I strongly suggest that you keep in mind that given that there is no space between anything in this life it is ultimately impossible to break another without oneself likewise being broken.

Now if that's not poetic injustice, with a femme fatale pimpilicious twist, then I have absolutely no idea of what is.

PIMPILICIOUS, OR NOT?
KINGS OF PIMPS AND KINGS OF POP?

I shed a great many tears and did much contemplating and reminiscing of my childhood experiences and teachings as I initially composed this profile of Prince and Michael Jackson. Given all of the legends that passed before them, the passing of Prince and Michael Jackson distinctly marked the end of an era when Black people were collectively obsessed with being the absolute best at everything that we undertook. Both The Nelson and The Jackson Families brought my generation and I such an immeasurable amount of joy and inspiration throughout our lives and their music is in fact a very heartfelt and emotional part of the life experience of Black people collectively.

Being a grand inquisitor level master of the subject on which I am about to write I clearly realize that there are those who even given an eternity will simply never ever, ever comprehend the points that I am about to make or my reasons for making them.

Firstly, I offer my family's sincere condolences and apologies to The Nelson and Jackson Families for their great loss. I feel that it is extremely important that these points be made especially since I have been infuriated myself on the many occasions over the years when I have heard people say that Michael Jackson wasn't Black.

Michael Jackson was not only black, he was larger than Black, he was a Black Hole that sucked everything that got near it into it and kept it mesmerized by his spell for the entirety of his professional life and even in his death he has generated a dizzying array of totally unparalleled statistics that are directly related to his stellar accomplishments.

I have long wanted to write about what I have clearly perceived about the largess and unparalleled magnetism of Prince and Michael Jackson, however, out of respect for their status and the extremely sensitive nature of the work that they were faithfully carrying out during their lives I declined to write about my perceptions while they were alive and I only shared my realizations with other master pimps of various ranks, some of whom had a very difficult time realizing what I was trying to point out to them. However, in the end, there was not a single true master that I encountered and conversed with who failed to recognize the sheer capable genius of both once I pointed out the numerous completely incontrovertible parallels, profiles and factors which caused me to be completely convinced that both Prince and Michael Jackson were in Pimpnological fact prodigious and extremely highly accomplished master pimps.

Over the years several comedians made highly popular and lucrative comedy routines that characterized Michael Jackson as a pimp in some urban center like New York City being visited by his square older brother Tito. However, sometimes when people make jokes there is a grim reality that underlies them, and I believe that this was likewise true of Michael Jackson.

PIMPILICIOUS, OR NOT?
KINGS OF PIMPS AND KINGS OF POP?

Looking at the completely mind boggling level of influential frenzy that Prince' and Michael Jackson's presence inspired among both their fans and foes alike, one has to ask himself, what lies behind such a titanic force that was for so many of us a major component that rested firmly at the very center of our lives for so many decades?

My conclusion is a Black Hole!

Being from Memphis, TN., which a major religious center and a major center of Black religious teaching, "Comprehending Flow," which is the central and most revered, potent and by far the most ancient Black religious teaching that we have, which even I pass to my own children today, was a major component of our everyday lives when I was coming up. And music, being a major aspect of "Flow," was likewise a central part of our lives.

When I was a child, we were taught that Michael Jackson was a great master of "Flow" who was extremely precious to us and who was doing extremely important work for us (Black People) and we were highly encouraged to strive to master "Flow" and be great musicians like Michael Jackson ourselves. And in the deep Southern religious centers to complement us as children we were often told one of two things, we were either told that we looked a preacher or we were told that we looked like Michael Jackson, even if we looked nothing like him at all.

PIMPILICIOUS, OR NOT?
KINGS OF PIMPS AND KINGS OF POP?

This was so widespread in the Black community that when Michael Jackson started to have a series of reconstructive surgeries that at first made him appear White and eventually made him appear alien, Comedians started to make jokes that went "When I was a Child, people used to tell me that I looked like Michael Jackson, they don't say that sh** anymore!" Black America and much of the entirety of America itself laughed heartily at these jokes because they were truly a reality of our everyday lives.

I can recall that as a junior high school student one of my close friend's uncle was a limousine driver and he was to be the driver for Michael Jackson, his uncle became an instant celebrity figure, everyone wanted to hear his story, we heard about this for years on end after that, as though he had been a driver for the Christ himself. In his death, I have come to think of Michael Jackson as our Gandhi.

As to the highly controversial points of this profile of Prince and Michael Jackson, which just as the other books in The Truth About Pimpology book series has specifically been composed for those who have an interest in understanding the real truth about the laws and truths of pimping, I started to suspect that something was super-normal about Michael Jackson during the Italian leg of one of his tours in the early 80's.

At the time I was an eleven year old child in the ghettos of Chicago, IL. And I can clearly recall marveling at the

PIMPILICIOUS, OR NOT?
KINGS OF PIMPS AND KINGS OF POP?

television set as I watched this Black man dressed like a military figure being followed around by a squad of Italian Special Forces troops in formation as he jogged around the city. Needless to say it was a stunning sight. Michael Jackson looked like the Grand Commander of the Rhythm Nation's Pop Army. That image was quite amazing to me and it stayed with me for years, even to this day, thirty six years later.

Later that year my family moved to Minneapolis, MN, which was then one of North America's premier prostitution centers and I met Prince and Andre Cymone skating around Lake Calhoun and got both their autographs and I soon became an apprentice to a master pimp from West Memphis, AR. and I again started to be passed the laws of "Flow" as I had all of my life. However, this time I was not receiving the law merely as required ancient lectures, this time I was studying them as they applied to pandering and prostitution as I was in training under a veteran master pimp in preparation for a career as a master of law designation master pimp, but that image of Michael Jackson still stayed with me.

A few years later, after I moved back home to Memphis, TN., and mastered comprehension of many other extremely vital aspects of "Flow" under the guidance of my grandfather, mostly during fishing trips to Mississippi, I can remember that I was at a book store when I was 19 and I happened upon a children's book written by Michael Jackson just after the Berlin Wall came down.

PIMPILICIOUS, OR NOT?
KINGS OF PIMPS AND KINGS OF POP?

I picked the book up and read a few passages and found myself crying in stunned disbelief at the inconceivably high level of comprehension of "Flow" that the book contained. I bought the book and took it home and studied it closely, it was at this point that I realized without question that the only person who could have this level of comprehension of these aspects of the laws of the ancient Black religion had to be an extremely high ranking master pimp; absolutely no one else studies these laws from these aspects except pimps.

By this point in my life, after having spent the vast majority of my life being highly indoctrinated in the laws of "Flow" and having spent years as the apprentice of numerous master pimps and those who had awareness of the ideology and tactics employed by pimps alike, I very clearly recognized that both Prince and Michael Jackson had several behavioral and lifestyle patterns that were directly parallel to those of master pimps and I started to observe them closely.

The living miracles of Prince and Michael Jackson, the child prodigy and pimp aficionado who specialized in black magic and sonic warfare in the form of what eventually came to be known as "Soul Sonic Force," are far deeper and more complex than those who don't know of the philosophy that drove progressive Black people of the time can comprehend.

I was only able to recognize these patterns myself because I was brought up under the same principles of "Flow" that they and many other musicians employed to wage an ultra-soft counter-offensive against division, hatred and discrimination and because I am far beyond a master profiler of panderers and prostitutes, as a matter of upbringing, habit, training, and ultimately life sustaining necessity, I am able to make very accurate determinations about exactly who is and who is not a panderer or prostitute and I have displayed this capability for many skeptics in both the worlds of organized crime and law enforcement alike over the years.

As I methodically observed how the entirety of both Prince' and Michael Jackson's profiles, lifestyle patterns, accomplishments, visible mentors, total obsession with White women, and ultimately their final tragic fates very specifically directly paralleled those of Blaxploitation Era Pimps I was able to very clearly determine that possessing this many clear parallels to Blaxploitation Era Pimps would be completely impossible without Prince and Michael Jackson in fact having been Blaxploitation Era Pimps themselves. And while I cannot officially declare that Prince and Michael Jackson were a given level of master pimp (as though they'd go down in some pimp hall of fame that doesn't exist), they both had far too many factors in their life experience that directly paralleled those of a Blaxploitation Era Pimp for me to believe that they weren't.

For the record, I think that it is important to note that I have never mis-profiled anyone who fit a given profile on three strong points; many of you might find it quite interesting that since the dramatic shift in his lifestyle, image and artistic approach that occurred in about 1979 or so our man Michael Jackson matched the profile of a master pimp on twenty five points. And listed below are twenty five factors to support my profiles conclusions.

1) The core primary aim of any true master pimp is to win souls and convince as many individuals as possible that they can't live without him, to completely convince his subjects that the world is flat and if they get too far away from his pimping they will walk off of the edge of the world and Michael Jackson unquestionably had the souls of legions of people all around the world. A pimp wants to capture souls, redirect subconscious minds and completely reshape entire destinies and Michael Jackson was able to accomplish this core pimp objective to a greater geographical extent than anyone in recorded history ever had before him including the Caesars, Hitler, Elvis and anyone else who has wielded global influence.

2) Another core objective of pimps is to get inside of people's heads and move things around. Given that real Black people, and subsequently real Black pimps, don't believe in the power of the conscious mind our entire academic focus is on learning how to affectively subliminalize people. Coincidentally, Michael Jackson's single greatest feat was that he was able to completely warp the entire world's concept of reality with the subliminal

messages in songs like "Rock with you" and "You are not alone". Through them he made himself immortal in people's subconscious minds and many people (including myself) didn't realize that we thought that he could not die.

Music has the power to reach deep into people's subconscious minds and rhythm and movements have the power to act as powerfully reinforcing mnemonics and through his music Michael Jackson had spent years enforcing and enforcing and positively reinforcing that "Love would survive and we would rock forever" and we didn't believe this...we just knew it in the deepest recesses of our minds.

The mind cannot resist evidence, and since Michael Jackson had been a permanent fixture in many of our lives for the vast majority of our lives and we had spent decades being absolutely assured that he would always be there it will take years for us to truly believe that he in fact really is dead.

3) Many of the visible mentors in Michael Jackson's life like Quincy Jones also had unmistakable parallels of pimps and so did their mentors (like "Bump") that were mentioned in books that I have read about them, which would have made Michael Jackson at least a 3rd generation lineage master pimp.

4) Michael Jackson had a very classic pattern of dysfunction within his family including accusations of child molestation that spanned generations; these are also very common direct parallels of pimps.

5) Like most pimps, Michael Jackson absolutely loved children and was trapped in the adolescent phase of life preferring to spend his days at Disney World with children, possibly attempting to relive his stolen childhood, than doing the things of a normal grown man. Being abnormally childish and being trapped within adolescence is also a very common pattern of pimps.

6) Alternative Education: It was often said that Michael Jackson did not have a proper education. However, many lineage master pimps are so highly indoctrinated in the ancient laws of "Flow" that they have little faith in or regard for any other form of enlightenment.

7) Part of Michael Jackson's family was from Alabama, which is a major center of pimps which breeds, educates, equips and dispatches true master pimps all over the world; Gary, IN. and Detroit, MI., were also major Blaxploitation Era pandering and prostitution centers.

8) Like many urban pimps, Michael Jackson was oddly and extremely extravagant in every aspect of his life. Who do

you know of who has had a chimp named Bubbles and an amusement park in their back yard?

And his wardrobe, I have written that a pimp is a dream policeman who should be placed under arrest by the m*****f***ing fashion police. While Mike's outfits (which were often signature pimp red and black) weren't quite as funny farm intern tasteless as that of many Chicago area pimps of the seventies era were, Mike should have at least been put under round the clock fashion police surveillance.

9) Drug Addiction: Michael Jackson is said to have had an addiction to prescription drugs and, just as the rich and famous always have, kept a doctor at his side to prescribe them to him. It is even suspected that he died of a drug overdose. Anyone who knows anything at all about pimping knows that the pimp and the dope dealer are inseparable partners and pharmacists and physicians are ultimately nothing more than dope dealers with licenses.

10) 360 Degree Departure: Given that the world is round and it turns, much like true Black people, true Black pimps tend to view things from a circuitous, as opposed to a linear, perspective and much like the overwhelming majority of pimps that have exercised over the millennia Mike arrived on the scene with nothing and departed it hundreds of millions of dollars in debt. The fact that you enter and leave

this life with absolutely nothing is the law and an insurmountable pattern of pimping.

11) Gross Inability To Relate To Men: Pimps invariably have extremely feminine characteristics and feel closer to their mothers and completely alienated from male figures in general. Pimps generally fear, distrust and have absolutely no ability whatsoever to relate to other men; especially their fathers, whom they have often never known or feel that they've never known.

12) Unstable Interracial Relationships: This is a definite and very common profile of pimps that is generally the result of having been severely appalled or rejected by their own race of women.

13) Extreme Counter-rejection, Especially, Of Women: Many pimps have a desperate need to completely win and then completely reject the most beautiful, shapely, wealthy and in general highly sought-after of women. Pimps have what many people don't realize is an extremely desperate need to bow the most awesome of women and reduce them to worthless piles of trash.

14) Illusions Of Grandeur: Attempting to elevate oneself high above others while demoralizing and thinking absolutely nothing of others is a very common and extremely unhealthy pattern of pimps. In true master pimp ideology it

is taught that reality is determined by focus and reality is a projection of that which exists in the mind, it is taught that you cannot sell anyone anything or make anyone believe anything that you don't buy yourself and resultantly a pimp must first become King in the deepest recesses of his subconscious mind to become King in fact.

15) A Desperate Need For Praise And Affirmation: This is yet another sign that one has a deep seated inferiority complex which is in fact a very common pattern among extremely successful people. Over the years I have encountered many individuals who have a constant need to do things to gain a tremendous amount of praise and affirmation from people.

16) Surrogate Family: Many members of the pimp culture and other underworld cultures prefer surrogate family, such as wife-in-laws instead of real wives, over their biological family.

17) Exotic Sanctuaries: In Pimps: The Raw Truth, I said that pimps and whores run together because they are escapees from the morbid realities of their lives. I have been to many pimp's dwellings over the decades and they always contain bongs, drugs, psychedelic lights, curtains made of beads, exotic animals, waterfalls or some other escapist accessories that are clearly the product of a cannabis clouded judgment;

however, no pimp's lair that I have ever encountered has been quite like The Neverland Ranch.

18) Shocking And Distant: Pimps and whores are completely obsessed with being shocking, distant, and totally incomprehensible to people and they are often highly shunned and demoralized as a direct result of their isolationist cultural and behavioral patterns.

19) An Obsession With Cultural Reform: Pimps and whores are invariably rebels who much like all rebels are absolutely and completely dissatisfied with everything in their lives; no matter what comes along they want to conquer, redefine and reform it.

20) Imperial Regalia: Many pimps are obsessed with lions, crowns, crests, thrones and other imperial and military regalia. Pimps are also often highly influenced by brutal and completely irrational military extremists such as Hitler.

21) Competitive Insanity: Many people who have extreme inferiority complexes are completely obsessed with outdoing and receiving more praise and recognition than anyone around them.

22) Total Inability To Love Oneself: Many people who desperately love other people have absolutely no ability whatsoever to love themselves. In the case of pimps, they

generally love their mother, family or surrogate family far more than they love themselves.

23) Extreme Loneliness: Many pimps and people who play on women for a living and have countless women pleading for their time and companionship often complain of feelings of extreme loneliness.

24) Obsessive Image Consciousness: Another extremely feminine pattern of pimps, and a sign that one has a deep underlying inferiority complex, is that one is not satisfied with oneself and one's appearance. Though one looks great and makes oneself look even better one is always convinced that they can look even better until they eventually evolve into freaks.

25) Methodical Self-mutilation: Many people who suffer from extreme self-hatred are prone to injuring themselves through the use of drugs, self-mutilation or other forms of self-inflicted injury or punishment. And then there was Michael Jackson, who could afford to have others cut him.

With full realization of the fact that there is an extremely thin line between love and hate, I always viewed the series of surgeries that Michael Jackson underwent as a form of self-mutilation, as a sign that he had somehow been crushed, contorted and reformed into an apparent white supremacist; he appeared to me to be an extremely complex form of master victim, a living crucifix of sorts. However, in his defense, I must say that though reconstructive surgeons may have managed to make Mike look like Skeletor's extremely gifted baby brother just before his passing they never even once did a procedure on Mike that made him look like he had been trapped within the inescapable confines of a wind tunnel as has been the case with many reconstructive surgery patients.

As for Prince, Prince was Pimpnological in the fact that he sold so much raw sexual energy and imagery, including the image of a sizable penis on the cover of his highly controversial 1999 Album, that he is actually almost singlehandedly responsible for the devising and global implementation of parental advisory labels on media products.

1) Sex: Pimps invariably sell sex, and absolutely no one in the music world sold more raw sexual energy and imagery than Prince.

2) Insane Confidence: During his nearly forty year career, it was constantly mentioned that Prince was an extremely highly confident individual who always had absolutely no question in his mind that both he and his various undertakings would succeed. Even as a teenager, I immediately recognized this as a psychological profile of a

PIMPILICIOUS, OR NOT?
KINGS OF PIMPS AND KINGS OF POP?

Pimp, as Pimps are completely motivationally insane and invariably teach motivational insanity to their disciples.

3) Prodigious: Pimps are totally relentless hardcore predators for sharp young disciples to pass their ism and ideology to and one absolutely must be witty and strong minded to take on and attempt to master The Pimping, because pimping is like The Torah in that, you either master The Torah or you lose your mind.

Many individuals have totally lost their minds trying to master the pimping without proper guidance.

4) Prettier Than A Woman: Given that Pimps invariably think that they're pretty and Blacks are one of the only races on Earth whose men look far better than our women, Pimps invariably look better than the women around them and in the case of Prince I cannot recall a single case when Prince didn't look and dress exponentially better than any of the women around him.

5) Regular At The Beauty Salon: Much like pimps, these guys were regulars at the beautician…

Pimps absolutely must shine and recline!

6) Flashy Clothing: Not only are Pimps into Flashy Clothing, Pimps are into having their own exclusive colors as signature

identifying markers, exactly as Prince did with the imperial color Purple that Prince made his own.

There has never ever been a woman that ever walked the face of this Earth who loved or spent more money on clothing than a Pimp; myself, very much included. As for the high heels, many of you fake fashion aficionados out there probably aren't aware that it was in fact Aristocratic Frenchmen who actually wore high heels first and then heels eventually evolved into an exclusively female fashion accessory.

7) Suspected Homosexuality: Just as many Pimps, both Prince and Michael Jackson were long suspected of being homosexual or bisexual.

8) Relationship Dysfunctional: Unfortunately, it is a mortal character flaw, specifically of urban pimps, that urban pimps are almost invariably relationship dysfunctional and as soon as I heard that our little Purple Friend was found dead in his compound, I thought to myself that, what made him had inevitably broken him...

The initial miracle of Prince was that he did everything by himself and he theoretically didn't need anyone else and was largely self-isolationist. However, as is so often the case, self-isolationism proved to be a death sentence, because if he had had a wife or even a personal caretaker, you wouldn't be reading this book right now and we would still be marveling at his astounding whit and boundless creativity.

9) Tremendous Faith In And Support From Women: Like a Pimp, Prince had tremendous faith in women and constantly befriended them, employed them, kept himself surrounded by them and was heavily supported by women.

10) Magnetic To Whores: Like many Pimps, Prince was extremely attractive to women but he was extremely highly magnetic to whores and other promiscuous women.

11) Complaints Of Loneliness: Like many Urban Pimps, as opposed to far more solid, long term married, totally family and surrogate family oriented Rural Pimps, Prince complained of loneliness when he felt that he wasn't being productive, even though he was surrounded by women.

12) Apparently Obsessed With Sex, But Doesn't Engage In It: During Prince' stellar career, he was apparently obsessed with the subject of sex, but he was not commonly known to have actually engaged in much of it… Like many Pimps and Whores, he merely used sex as a means to an end, but he wasn't publicly known to actually engage in much of it.

13) A Devout Leisurologist: Even though His Royal Badness was known as an absolutely relentless work-a-holic, in personal quotes and in some of his movie scripts, he

espoused the ancient Pimpnological Philosophy that he never felt that he had worked a single day and he didn't do anything professionally, he only did things for fun.

14) Product Of A Hardcore Human Trafficking Center: Much like myself, Prince was a product of A Hardcore Human Trafficking Center.

As a matter of fact, we are products of one of exactly the same Human Trafficking Centers, because while he was building a career for himself, I was in Uptown riding up and down The Lake Street Track everyday being trained to read and monitor Whores and the Police as I was being to trained to Pimp everyday on the exact same track that he famously wrote about.

15) Childish And Comedic: Believe it or not, one very common and easily recognizable marker of Pimps is that they are invariably childish and comedic in nature; albeit, sadistically comedic in some cases.

16) Restless and Sporadic: Pimps have to keep moving or traveling somewhere or cruising around analyzing something.

17) Club Ownership: Many Pimps own bars, clubs, restaurants and other night spots.

PIMPILICIOUS, OR NOT?
KINGS OF PIMPS AND KINGS OF POP?

18) Likes To Throw Parties: Pimps absolutely live and breathe to Pimp, Party, Parade!

19) Highly Creative: Pimps are invariably highly creative people, whether it is making music, making themselves believe that they look better than everybody else or whether they are pimping whores with an HVAC License, Pimps tend to be very creative.

20) Accomplishes The Impossible: Pimps always accomplish what other people think is impossible.

21) Interracial Dating: Pimps almost always date and marry outside of their race.

22) Mysterious: Pimps are invariably a great mystery to people.

23) Loves Music: Pimps absolutely love mood and meditation music.

24) Superiority Complex: Since Pimps view themselves as Kings of The Concrete Jungle who have women taking care of them exactly like The Lion who is The King Of The Jungle, while the average Joe on the street can't get a woman to do anything for him except keep them broke and with a migraine headache, Pimps invariably have totally huge superiority complexes.

25) Territorial Conflicts With Other Pimps: Prince and Michael Jackson never seemed to want to admit that there was stiff competition induced conflict between them. However, just like a couple of Pimps, they were apparently in extreme territorial conflict for the title of King Of Pop, an apparent conflict that sales statistically, the far more highly trained and insanely motivated and dedicated traditional Pimp parallel Michael Jackson won by virtually every measure, even after his death. However, Prince was no slouch... He was a legendary creative dynamo that could only be compared to the likes of Salvador Dali or Mozart.

While Prince was perceived as being full on sexually explicit, Michael Jackson was merely edgy and resultantly far more globally commercially viable. Michael Jackson also very shrewdly had the masterful business sense to reproduce and subsequently re-sales cycle Thriller and other works and invest in highly valuable music rights and entire catalogs of music that he could easily monetize like The Beatles Catalog that he owned and he had the uncommon business sense to invest heavily in something that he actually understood.

While all of the previous points may sound like pure speculation to many of you, they are far too coincidental for me. It is my far beyond professional opinion that there is absolutely no way that any individual can have that many direct parallels that are solely exclusive to Blaxploitation Era Pimps and not be A Blaxploitation Era Pimp.

PIMPILICIOUS, OR NOT?
KINGS OF PIMPS AND KINGS OF POP?

If Prince and Michael Jackson weren't pimps they sure did have a large number of profiles that evenly parallel those of pimps and they had been using an exceptional number of high level pimp tactics that you absolutely cannot gain through mere casual association.

Of course, unfortunately both Prince and Michael Jackson are no longer alive to verify or refute my conclusions, but one thing is for sure, and that is that True Master Pimps will lay claim to both Prince and Michael Jackson for years to come, as a matter of fact for as long as their names ring around the world, even until they inevitably fade into the annals of mythology, for surely no one who did not live in their time will ever believe the sheer mass of their totally inconceivably stellar accomplishments.